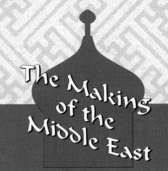

The Making of the Middle East

Tensions in the Gulf 1978-1991

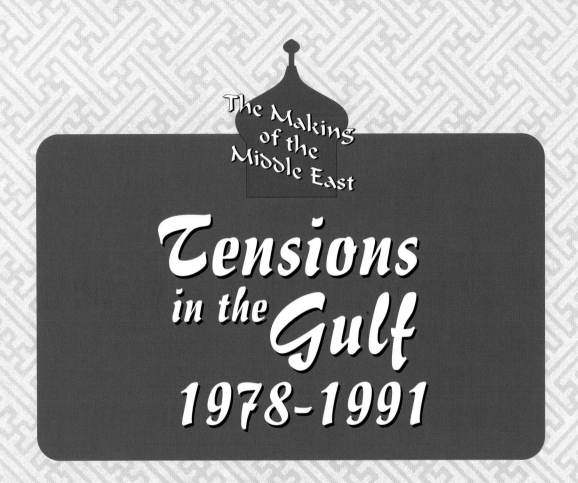

The Making of the Middle East

Tensions in the Gulf 1978-1991

J. E. Peterson

Mason Crest Publishers
Philadelphia

Frontispiece: Iraqi tanks destroyed during the 1991 Gulf War.

Produced by OTTN Publishing, Stockton, N.J.

Mason Crest Publishers
370 Reed Road
Broomall, PA 19008
www.masoncrest.com

First printing

1 3 5 7 9 8 6 4 2

Library of Congress Cataloging-in-Publication Data

  Peterson, John, 1947–
    Tensions in the Gulf, 1978–1991 / J. E. Peterson.
        p. cm. — (The making of the Middle East)
    Includes bibliographical references and index.
    ISBN-13: 978-1-4222-0175-6
    ISBN-10: 1-4222-0175-9
   1. Persian Gulf Region—History—Juvenile literature. 2. Iran—History—1979–1997—Juvenile literature.
  3. Iran-Iraq War, 1980–1988—Juvenile literature. 4. Persian Gulf War, 1991—Juvenile literature I. Title.
    DS247.A138P48 2007
    953.6—dc22
                            2007024594

Table of Contents

Introduction:
The Importance of the Middle East

The region known as the Middle East has a significant impact on world affairs. The countries of the greater Middle East—the Arab states of the Arabian Peninsula, Eastern Mediterranean, and North Africa, along with Israel, Turkey, Iran, and Afghanistan—possess a large portion of the world's oil, a valuable commodity that is the key to modern economies. The region also gave birth to three of the world's major faiths: Judaism, Christianity, and Islam.

In recent years it has become obvious that events in the Middle East affect the security and prosperity of the rest of the world. But although such issues as the wars in Iraq and Afghanistan, the floundering Israeli-Palestinian peace process, and the struggles within countries like Lebanon and Sudan are often in the news, few Americans understand the turbulent history of this region.

Human civilization in the Middle East dates back more than 8,000 years, but in many cases the modern conflicts and issues in the region can be attributed to events and decisions made during the past 150 years. In particular, after World War I ended in 1918, the victorious Allies—especially France and Great Britain—redrew the map of the Middle East, creating a number of new countries, such as Iraq, Jordan, and Syria. Other states, such as Egypt and Iran, were dominated by foreign powers until after the Second World War. Many of the Middle Eastern countries did not become independent until the 1960s or 1970s. Political and economic developments in the Middle Eastern states over the past four decades have shaped the region's direction and led to today's headlines.

The purpose of the MAKING OF THE MIDDLE EAST series is to nurture a better understanding of this critical region, by providing the basic history along

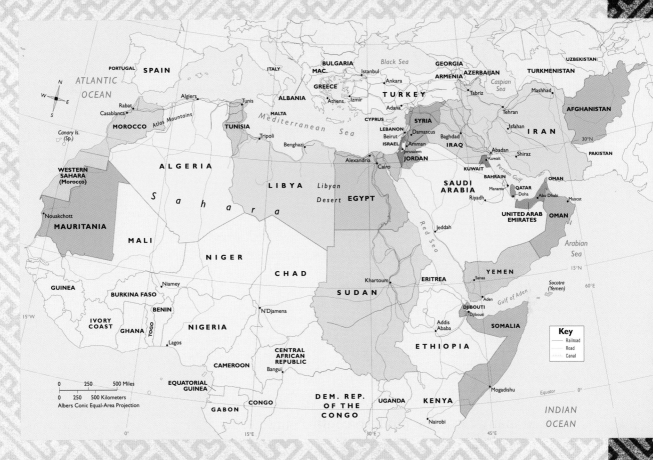

with explanation and analysis of trends, decisions, and events. Books will examine important movements in the Middle East, such as the development of nationalism in the 1880s and the rise of Islamism from the 1970s to the present day.

The 10 volumes in the MAKING OF THE MIDDLE EAST series are written in clear, accessible prose and are illustrated with numerous historical photos and maps. The series should spark students' interest, providing future decision-makers with a solid foundation for understanding an area of critical importance to the United States and the world.

(Opposite) An oil refinery in Rabigh, Saudi Arabia. The countries of the Persian Gulf hold about half of the world's petroleum reserves, giving the region enormous economic and strategic importance. (Right) A scene from the hajj, the annual pilgrimage of Muslims to Mecca. The vast majority of the Gulf's 130 million people are adherents of Islam.

1 *Overview*

The Tigris and Euphrates Rivers, which nurtured some of the world's first civilizations, meet near the present-day Iraqi town of Al Qurnah. The combined river, known as the Shatt al Arab, flows southeastward for about 120 miles (193 kilometers) before emptying into a body of water that holds enormous strategic importance for modern civilization. Throughout most of the globe, that body of water is known as the Persian Gulf, though Arab states insist it should properly be called the Arabian Gulf.

Stretching some 550 miles (885 km) southeastward to the Strait of Hormuz, a narrow waterway that connects it to the Gulf of Oman—and beyond, to the open waters of the Arabian Sea—the Persian Gulf is about 200 miles (322 km) at its widest point. Its warm waters lap the coastlines of eight states: Iran, Iraq, Kuwait, Saudi Arabia, Bahrain, Qatar, the United Arab Emirates, and Oman. Together these countries are believed to hold more than half of the world's reserves of petroleum—the fuel that makes modern economies run—and each year they supply in excess of one-quarter of the worldwide demand. For this reason, what happens in the Gulf region is of enormous importance throughout the world.

The Persian Gulf region, like the Middle East overall, has experienced significant political tension and conflict. During the period 1978–1991, the Gulf witnessed a series of tumultuous events—including the Islamic Revolution in Iran and two major wars—that reverberated throughout the Middle East and beyond. To a considerable degree, the consequences of those events are still being felt today.

The Countries of the Gulf and Their Peoples

Seven of the eight states surrounding the Gulf—Iran is the exception—are Arab countries. In all of the Gulf countries, the vast majority of the people follow Islam, though they may belong to either the Sunni or Shia branch of the faith. Politically, six of the Gulf states—Saudi Arabia, Kuwait, the United Arab Emirates, Bahrain, Oman, and Qatar—remain conservative monarchies. Iran is a conservative theocracy, while Iraq is in transition after decades of dictatorial rule by Saddam Hussein. Although all the Gulf states produce oil, material conditions vary markedly. In some of the smaller states, oil revenues have been sufficient to raise the standard of living of

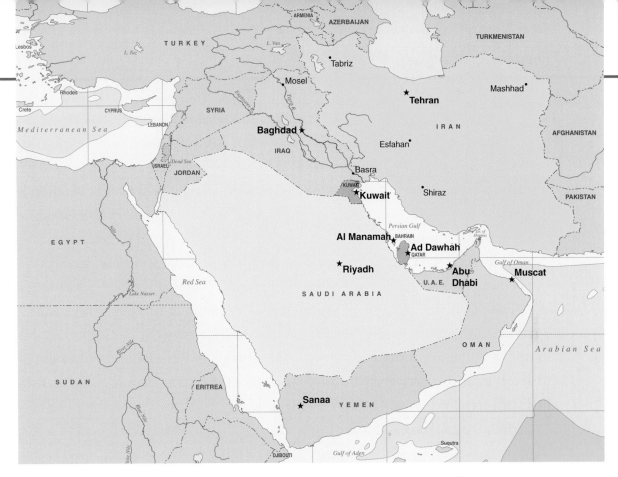

This map shows the eight countries that border the Persian Gulf.

virtually everyone. In the larger states, however, many people are still poor.

Iran, formerly known as Persia, is by far the Gulf's most populous country. In 2006 it was home to an estimated 68.6 million people, of whom more than half were ethnic Persians. Iran also has a sizable Azeri minority, along with smaller communities of ethnic Kurds, Lurs, Arabs, Baluch, Turkmen, and others. With more than 7 million residents, Tehran, the national capital, is the largest city in the Gulf.

Nearly all Iranians are Muslims, and about 9 in 10 of them belong to the Shia branch of Islam, which broke away from the main body of Muslims, the Sunnis, centuries ago. (Today Sunnis account for about 80 to 85 percent of all Muslims worldwide.) Other religions that claim smaller numbers of adherents in Iran are Christianity, Zoroastrianism (an ancient religion of Persia), Baha'i (a religion that originated in Persia during the 19th century), and Judaism.

Although it supports many industries, Iran remains a largely rural country where agriculture employs some 3 in 10 workers. The country has large deposits of natural gas, but oil production is the engine that drives Iran's economy. Unfortunately, oil exports have been stagnant for decades, and the country's growing population means that for many the economic situation is bleak; according to a recent estimate, 40 percent of Iranians may live below the poverty line.

Oil exports have been anything but stagnant in Saudi Arabia, the Gulf's largest country by area. In fact, Saudi Arabia is the world's largest oil exporter. It also holds about 25 percent of the world's proven oil reserves.

An estimated 27 million people were living in Saudi Arabia in 2006, making it the Gulf's second most populous state. However, at least 5.5 million of these people were foreigners residing and working in the country, mostly in the oil and service sectors. Along with South Asians and Southeast Asians, these expatriates included people from other parts of the Arab world as well as Westerners.

The Saudi government considers itself the guardian of Islam's holiest sites—the religion arose, in the seventh century A.D., on territory that is now part of Saudi Arabia—and today all Saudi citizens are Muslims. Perhaps 10 percent of the population is Shia; the rest follow a conservative form of Sunni Islam that is known outside Saudi Arabia as Wahhabism. It forbids the worship of saints, the consumption of tobacco and alcohol, and the playing of music and other entertainments. Wahhabism also insists on the strict separation of men and women in all public settings. Because of its influence, Saudi Arabia is the most conservative country in the Gulf region.

The Kingdom of Saudi Arabia was created in 1932 under the leadership of the Al Saud family, which had been prominent in the interior of the Arabian Peninsula since the 18th century. Before the discovery of oil in the 1930s, Saudi Arabia was one of the world's poorest countries. But oil revenues funded the country's rapid development, particularly from the 1950s on.

For more than 60 years, the United States and Saudi Arabia have maintained a "special relationship." In 1945 the two countries' respective leaders, President Franklin Delano Roosevelt and King Abd al-Aziz, met aboard an American ship in the Suez Canal and reached a secret agreement. In return for access to Saudi oil, the United States would guarantee Saudi Arabia's security, protecting the kingdom from potential enemies. Over the years, the United States has purchased billions of dollars of Saudi oil, and the Saudis have used much of that money to buy American weapons systems, oil-drilling equipment, communications systems, and infrastructure-development services.

Saudi Arabia's northern neighbor Iraq has the world's second largest petroleum reserves. And with an estimated 2006 population of about 26.7 million, Iraq is roughly the same size as Saudi Arabia. But conditions in the two Gulf nations are dramatically different. Iraq's economy has been battered

U.S. president Franklin Delano Roosevelt (right) meets with Abd al-Aziz ibn Saud, the king of Saudi Arabia, aboard the USS *Quincy*, February 14, 1945. Recognizing the strategic importance of Saudi Arabia's vast oil reserves, Roosevelt pledged that the United States would guarantee the kingdom's security.

by the 2003 U.S.-led invasion that toppled the regime of Saddam Hussein, and by the internal violence that has raged ever since. Oil production remains well below capacity, vital infrastructure is in shambles, jobs are scarce, and living standards are low.

Like Iran, Iraq has a diverse population. About three-quarters of the people are ethnic Arabs, up to 20 percent are Kurds, and the remainder are of

Turkman, Assyrian, or other extraction. Iraq has small Christian communities as well as some Jews, but the overwhelming majority of Iraqis—approximately 97 percent—are Muslims. However, the country is deeply divided between the Arab Shia, who make up a majority of the population, dominate the government established after the 2003 U.S.-led invasion, and are concentrated especially in the south; the Sunni Arabs, who were in control before 2003 and are concentrated in the middle of the country; and the Sunni Kurds, who had set up their own autonomous zone in northern Iraq in the decade before Saddam Hussein's fall.

The remaining five Gulf states are all small. Oman, the largest of the five by area (though it has only a very short coastline on the Gulf) and by population, was home to an estimated 3.1 million people in 2006. Tiny Bahrain, which is made up of more than 30 islands off Saudi Arabia's eastern shore, had a 2006 population of approximately 700,000. All of the smaller Gulf states have sizable populations of foreign workers. For example, slightly more than half of the 2.4 million people living in Kuwait—which borders Iraq and Saudi Arabia—are non-nationals. In Qatar the proportion is even higher: an estimated 80 percent of the 885,000 people residing in the country, located on a peninsula that juts out into the Gulf near Bahrain, are foreign workers. Likewise, in the United Arab Emirates (UAE)—a union of seven small traditional states, the most important of which are Abu Dhabi and Dubai—expatriates make up about 8 in 10 residents.

Among citizens of Oman, the UAE, Kuwait, Qatar, and Bahrain, Arab Sunni Muslims make up the majority. There are, however, smaller groups of Persians and Shia Muslims.

All five states produce and export oil. Kuwait and Abu Dhabi have enormous reserves, but Bahrain's oil is nearly finished and Oman's production is modest. Qatar has one of the world's largest deposits of natural gas. The five states are members, along with Saudi Arabia, of an organization known as the Gulf Cooperation Council, and they are all tied politically and economically to the West. All have hereditary leaders, known as emirs or, in the case of Oman, a sultan.

The British in the Persian Gulf

During the 19th and early 20th century, Britain gained great influence in the Gulf region—so great, in fact, that some commentators referred to the Gulf as a "British lake." Beginning in the 1800s, the British—who sought to keep the Gulf shipping route open and to lock European rivals out of the region—concluded a series of treaties with local rulers on the Arab side of the Gulf. Ultimately the smaller states along the western shores of the Gulf—while remaining formally independent—would yield control of their foreign affairs and defense to Britain, and the British also influenced the decisions taken by their rulers. During World War I (1914–1918) the British also established a protectorate over the central Arabian lands of the Al Saud. In return Abd al-Aziz ibn Saud, the Al Saud's leader, pledged to attack local allies of the Turkey-based Ottoman Empire, a British enemy in World War I. (Abd al-Aziz would later unify Saudi Arabia under his rule.) Also during the First World War, the British conquered the Ottoman territory of Mesopotamia (present-day Iraq), which they governed after the war under a mandate from the newly established League of Nations.

A column of British soldiers on the march in the Ottoman province of Mesopotamia, circa 1917. During World War I, British forces won control of the province, which was renamed Iraq. Between 1920 and 1932, Britain administered Iraq under a League of Nations mandate.

In Iran, meanwhile, the British had long vied for control with Russia. The two imperial powers finally signed an agreement in 1907 that acknowledged Russian influence in northern Iran and British influence in southern and eastern Iran. Two years later, the Anglo-Persian Oil Company was set up to develop Iran's recently discovered oil fields. The British government acquired a majority stake in the company because Iranian oil was critical to plans to convert the Royal Navy from a coal-powered to an oil-powered force.

The powerful British presence in the Gulf, and much of the rest of the Middle East, declined after World War II (1939–1945), when many states in the region became independent. Over the following decades, the British gradually abandoned their military bases in the Middle East.

In 1968 the British government announced its intention to close its remaining bases in the Persian Gulf and withdraw from the region by 1971. British treaty obligations to protect the smaller Gulf states would end, and those states would gain full independence.

U.S.-Soviet Rivalry in the Gulf

In the aftermath of World War II, the United States and the Soviet Union, which had been wartime allies, emerged as bitter adversaries in a global struggle for ideological supremacy known as the Cold War. Eastern Europe's Communist nations were Soviet satellites, and the capitalist and democratic nations of Western Europe were firmly in the American camp, but elsewhere in the world the two sides scrambled to gather allies and thwart the designs of their enemy.

The strategically important Middle East was an area of particular concern for American policymakers. The West's support of Israel, which came into existence in 1948, drove many of the Arab states to look to the Soviet Union (and even to the Communist People's Republic of China) for assistance. Arab anger toward the West was further inflamed by an abortive British, French, and Israeli military incursion into Egypt in 1956.

U.S. officials had much to worry about in the oil-rich Persian Gulf. In Iraq the Soviet Union had forged close ties with the leftist rulers who had come to power in the years following the country's 1958 revolution, which overthrew the monarchy. The Soviets also provided the main support to leftist South Yemen (Aden) after its independence from the British in 1967. After it gained independence in 1961, Kuwait had signaled its Cold War neutrality by allowing Moscow to establish an embassy.

Elsewhere in the Gulf, however, the Soviets made few inroads. Iran had long been suspicious of the Soviet Union because of past Russian intrigues and Soviet attempts to create puppet Communist regimes in northern Iran during World War II. Saudi Arabia and the other smaller Gulf states had no ties with any Communist state. Omani officials complained about South Yemeni and Communist assistance to the liberation front active in the southern part of their country.

U.S. policymakers became increasingly worried about Soviet and Chinese activities in the Gulf during the 1970s. However, they were reluctant to directly commit U.S. forces in defense of the Gulf, in large part because of the difficult American experience in Vietnam. Instead, the United States tried to use Iran and Saudi Arabia as bulwarks against Communist expansion in the region. This was called the Twin Pillars strategy.

Iran's shah, or king, was eager to serve in this role. He spent a large amount of his country's revenues on his armed forces, building an arsenal of advanced weapons systems and equipment. He also sent troops to Oman to

American-made F-16 fighter jets at the Prince Sultan Air Base, near Al Kharj, Saudi Arabia. In the decades after World War II, Saudi Arabia used its massive oil revenues to purchase billions of dollars' worth of military equipment and infrastructure from the United States. American policy-makers hoped that the kingdom would serve as a bulwark against Communist expansion in the Gulf.

aid that country in its war against the Communist front. But Iran's role as one of the Twin Pillars was threatened as internal opposition to the shah grew.

Unlike Iran, Saudi Arabia did not have a large military force and would have had difficulty defending itself, let alone its neighbors. But it did buy billions of dollars of U.S. and European military equipment, and the United States helped train its forces and was permitted to keep some of its own equipment in the country. As Saudi Arabia was solidly anti-Communist, it provided other kinds of assistance to the West, especially financial support, during the Cold War.

By the end of the 1970s the Twin Pillars strategy of the United States was faltering. For the pro-U.S. Gulf states, Islamic extremism had become a greater threat than communism. Governments in the region were vulnerable to being overthrown by internal forces opposed to monarchy and alliances with the West.

(Right) Mohammad Reza Pahlavi, the shah of Iran, shakes hands with a U.S. Air Force general during a November 1977 trip to the United States. (Opposite) Ayatollah Ruhollah Khomeini greets supporters in Iran after 15 years in exile, February 1, 1979. Khomeini's Islamic Revolution toppled the shah's pro-Western regime and in its place established a conservative Shia theocracy.

2 The Iranian Revolution

In October 1971 a large collection of kings and queens, presidents and premiers, sheikhs, sultans, and other luminaries gathered near the ruins of the ancient city of Persepolis. Mohammad Reza Pahlavi, the shah of Iran, had invited these guests to a celebration of the 2,500th anniversary of the founding of the first Persian empire by Cyrus the Great. He spared no expense, spending up to $100 million on the construction of opulent accommodations, an army of French chefs, almost four tons of meat, and 25,000 bottles of wine.

The lavish party clearly had a purpose beyond simply honoring Cyrus the Great, who died in 529 B.C. The shah was attempting to connect his own rule with the grandeur of Persia's imperial past, to show that he was the latest in a long line of mighty Iranian kings and the legitimate ruler of his people.

The reality was a bit less glorious. The Pahlavi dynasty had been established in 1925 by the shah's father—an army officer and a commoner born Reza Khan—who had earlier seized power in a coup. Coronated as Reza Shah Pahlavi, he ruled until 1941. That year, in the midst of World War II, British and Soviet forces chased him from the throne for his pro-German leanings. Mohammad Reza Pahlavi, not yet 22 years old, became the new ruler of Iran.

In the early 1950s Iran's elected prime minister, Mohammad Mossadeq, attempted to constrain the shah's power and nationalize Iran's oil industry. After an apparently unsuccessful coup against Mossadeq by Iranian army officers, the shah briefly fled Iran in August 1953. With covert aid from the British and American intelligence services, however, pro-shah forces successfully ousted the prime minister, and the shah returned.

Even as he assembled a ruthless secret police apparatus to quash dissent, the shah charted a course of modernization for Iran. In 1963 he launched the so-called White Revolution. Oil

Mohammad Mosaddeq, Iran's prime minister, opposed the shah and sought to nationalize the Iranian oil industry. In August 1953, pro-shah forces overthrew Mosaddeq in a coup aided by the British and U.S. intelligence services.

revenues funded the ambitious reform program, which included industrial-ization and infrastructure building, large-scale agriculture projects, and expanded education. Women were given greater rights and freedoms, including the right to vote.

Not all Iranians were happy with the shah's reforms. In the countryside, rapid economic changes brought uncertainty and hardship. The *bazaaris*, small merchants and manufacturers, believed that economic modernization threatened their income and independence. Shia religious leaders and other conservative Muslims objected to the increasing Westernization and secular-ization of Iranian society, including more liberal attitudes toward women.

One Shia cleric, in particular, denounced the shah and his reform pro-gram. Ruhollah Khomeini, an ayatollah—a high-status leader in the Shia tra-dition—also condemned Iran's friendly relations with the United States and Israel. He was arrested and exiled to Turkey in 1964. Soon, however, he moved to the Shia holy city of Najaf, in Iraq. From there he continued to speak out against the shah.

Growing Opposition to the Shah

Throughout the remainder of the 1960s and into the 1970s, the shah plunged ahead with his campaign to modernize Iran. Through huge arms purchases, he also sought to make his country the Gulf's dominant military power and a guardian against Communist encroachment in the region.

But among growing numbers of Iranians, anger—at the shah's policies, at his increasingly harsh suppression of dissent, at the corruption and extrava-gant spending of the royal family—was simmering. By the late 1970s, various groups had begun organizing to oppose the shah politically. Loose alliances formed between leftists, Islamic leaders, the merchants, the middle class, and the masses of poor.

Opposition to the shah gained momentum in early 1978. Large demonstrations were held in several cities, some of them degenerating into bloody rioting. The prime minister was forced to resign. In September hundreds of people were killed when security forces fired into a crowd of some 20,000 demonstrators in Tehran. Further demonstrations and a series of strikes by petroleum workers cut oil production to a trickle, creating severe economic problems for the government. The shah appointed a military government, but it was unable to stop the unrest.

The shah's grip on power was slipping, but he seemed unable to take decisive action. Part of the explanation for this might have been his declining health: he was stricken with cancer.

One action the shah did take in 1978 backfired badly. He pressured the government of Iraq to expel Ayatollah Khomeini from Najaf. The Shia cleric—now the most visible symbol of resistance to the shah—went to France. In Paris he was better able to coordinate the opposition movement. Khomeini also enjoyed much greater media exposure in Paris. Followers recorded his sermons and speeches, and the cassette tapes were then smuggled into Iran, where they were broadcast to stir up further antagonism toward the shah's regime.

The Revolution Succeeds

On January 16, 1979, the ailing shah left Iran on what was described as an "extended vacation." In his absence, a violent struggle broke out between

Iranians' resentment of the shah had multiple causes, including his ruthless suppression of dissent, economic and social dislocations brought about by his modernization program, corruption in the royal family, and the increasing secularization of Iranian society. As opposition to the regime gained momentum in 1978, however, more and more Iranians began to rally around Shia religious leaders. These demonstrators in Tehran are carrying a placard of Ayatollah Mahmoud Taleghani, a prominent Shia cleric.

supporters of Khomeini, supporters of the shah, and supporters of the new prime minister, Shapour Bakhtiar, who sought to provide a middle path between the two camps.

On February 1, Khomeini returned triumphantly to Iran. He quickly appointed a provisional government, though it remained to be seen whether his supporters would actually emerge victorious in the struggle for power. Many Iranians feared that the military would intervene in support of the old regime. On February 9, however, elements of the armed forces mutinied, and by the following day the mutineers—bolstered by tens of thousands of civilian opponents of the shah and supporters of Khomeini—were battling loyalist forces on the streets of Tehran. On February 11 the military officially declared that it would not intervene in the struggle for power. With that the shah's cause collapsed completely. Ayatollah Khomeini's Islamic Revolution had triumphed.

Nevertheless, much of the country remained in a state of near chaos. There was as yet no effective central authority to replace the old regime. Revolutionary committees took over many regional and local functions, but they were essentially accountable to no one.

Political parties from varying points on the ideological spectrum sprang up, but Iran would not become a multiparty democracy. Instead the ayatollah and Shia religious officials—known as mullahs—quietly began consolidating their control. Khomeini assumed the role of *faqih*, or Supreme Leader of the revolution. Regarding himself as the representative of God, he did not believe he was constrained by any governmental authority. The Islamic Revolutionary Council, formed by Khomeini and dominated by mullahs who supported him, became the major center of political power. Revolutionary courts were established to judge members of the old system. Many people were sentenced to death, including the prime minister under the shah.

On April 1, 1979, following a national referendum, Ayatollah Khomeini declared Iran an Islamic republic. In the new constitution drafted later in the year, the goal of firmly rooting government and society in "Islamic principles" was central. To that end, various clauses ensured that, while Iran would have an elected president and legislature, or Majlis, the Shia clergy would exert decisive control over the political system. For instance, the unelected Guardian Council—composed of six clerics appointed directly by the Supreme Leader and six legal scholars appointed by an official appointed by the Supreme Leader—was given a range of powers, including the power to reject any candidate for elective office and the power to reject any legislation passed by the Majlis that it deemed un-Islamic.

Economically, the Iranian Revolution brought upheaval and hardship. Industry and agriculture were put under the control of religious figures rather than trained economists. A decline in oil production cut national income dramatically. Banks and major industries were nationalized, and the property of rich people was seized. As a result, production of many goods declined and shortages appeared.

Socially, the Islamic Revolution made Iran much more conservative and much less Western than it had been under the shah. Sharia, or Islamic law, became the basis of the country's legal system. In public women were compelled to wear the chador, a head-to-ankle dress. Education was segregated by gender. Men and women were forbidden to socialize publicly. Alcohol, foreign music, and other "decadent" influences from the West were banned. Morals offenders faced draconian punishments.

Not all of Iran's citizens were happy about living under a conservative Islamic theocracy. Many of Iran's non-Persian and non-Shia minorities demonstrated against these developments. Unrest in the provinces was violently put down.

Fearing a backlash by the military, Khomeini purged Iran's armed forces and created the Islamic Revolutionary Guards Corps. The mission of the Revolutionary Guards was to protect the revolution against internal threats.

Foreign Policy

Iran's hard-line new leaders did not believe that the Islamic Revolution should stop at the borders of their country. In their view, the mostly secular governments and Western-influenced societies of other Muslim countries in the region represented a betrayal of authentic Islam and should be swept away. To accomplish this the Iranian hard-liners sought to export their revolution.

Not surprisingly, this was an unsettling prospect for the leaders of neighboring Muslim countries. In the smaller Gulf states especially, enormous concern existed over the intentions of their larger, stronger, and now hostile neighbor. Bahrain, Kuwait, and Saudi Arabia all charged that Iran was actively helping opposition groups to organize and carry out subversive acts within their borders.

If Iran's efforts to export the Islamic Revolution badly strained relations with its Persian Gulf neighbors, a tense confrontation with the United States would lead to the complete severing of formal diplomatic relations between the two countries. In the months following the Islamic Revolution, U.S.-Iranian relations deteriorated steadily. Iran's new leaders regarded the United States—which they dubbed "the Great Satan"—as an imperialist intruder, both in their country and in the broader Middle East.

In October 1979 the U.S. government permitted the deposed shah of Iran to enter the United States to obtain treatment for his cancer. Iranians were outraged, and on November 4, a mob of militant students seized the U.S.

Militant Iranian students display a blindfolded American hostage following their November 4, 1979, seizure of the U.S. embassy in Tehran.

embassy in Tehran and took more than 60 diplomats and support staff hostage. They demanded that the shah be sent to Iran to face trial. The Iranian government made no effort to win release of the hostages; in fact, Ayatollah Khomeini praised the students' actions.

Jimmy Carter, the U.S. president, moved swiftly to impose sanctions. He stopped oil imports from Iran, halted shipment of American military parts,

Operation Eagle Claw—the ill-fated mission to rescue the American hostages being held in Tehran—began on the evening of April 24, 1980, with the launching of these helicopters from the U.S. aircraft carrier *Nimitz*. The mission had to be aborted the following day, after three helicopters developed mechanical problems. In the desert southeast of Tehran, one helicopter collided with a refueling plane, killing eight American servicemen.

and froze Iranian bank accounts in the United States. Although the Iranians did release 13 of the hostages, efforts to negotiate the release of the others went nowhere. In April 1980 Carter cut off diplomatic relations and approved a military operation to rescue the hostages. Mechanical failure forced the mission to be abandoned, however, and eight American servicemen were killed when a helicopter and a plane collided in the desert southeast of Tehran.

The standoff dragged on. After the shah's death in Cairo in July 1980, Ayatollah Khomeini announced that the hostages would be released if the United States agreed to certain conditions, including the return to Iran of assets held by the shah's family, the dropping of American financial claims against Iran, the release of frozen Iranian assets, a U.S. promise not to intervene in Iranian affairs, and a U.S. apology.

Although Ronald Reagan, the Republican candidate in the U.S. presidential election, agreed to most of the demands, President Carter refused to apologize to Iran. Reagan won the election, and the remaining 52 hostages were finally released only minutes after he took the oath of office on January 20, 1981.

Despite the release of the U.S. hostages, relations between the United States and Iran remained hostile. But by this time Iranian leaders had other issues to worry about. Their nation was at war.

(Opposite) A grisly scene from the Iran-Iraq War. The conflict caused upwards of a million casualties. (Right) When Iran and Iraq began targeting tankers of neutral countries, U.S. Navy vessels like those shown here began patrolling the Gulf to keep the shipping lanes open—and the oil flowing.

3 The Iran-Iraq War

The Islamic Revolution of 1979 helped spark an eight-year-long war between Iran and Iraq. But it cannot be said that the revolution was the only cause of the brutal conflict. Iran and Iraq had long been bitter rivals, and numerous issues had poisoned their relations with each other.

Background Tensions

From ancient times Arabs and Persians have viewed one another with suspicion. Arabs led the Islamic conquest of Persia in the eighth century. Persians conquered parts of the Arab world at various times before and after the emergence of Islam. More recently, Iran claimed Bahrain as a province until 1970. When the British withdrew from the Gulf the following year, Iran forcibly took over three small islands located near the entrance of the Gulf that were claimed by the United Arab Emirates.

Differences between Sunnis and Shia were another cause of friction between Iran and Iraq. Both countries had majority Shia populations, but in Iraq the Sunnis dominated government and society. Many Sunnis regard the Shia as having moved away from true Islam. Arab states of the Gulf charged that, since its revolution, Iran—the largest Shia country in the world—was actively encouraging Shia communities to oppose their governments.

Iran and Iraq also had long contended for status as the "great powers" of the Persian Gulf and competed with each other for influence in the region. The two countries promoted opposing ideologies. A decade after the overthrow of its monarchy in 1958, Iraq came to be dominated by the Arab socialist Baath Party. The shah's Iran, meanwhile, was Westernizing and capitalist. This difference reflected the two countries' relations with the superpowers: the Soviet Union supported Iraq, whereas the United States backed Iran.

Iran and Iraq also had a long history of border disputes. Most of Iran lies on an inland plateau separated from the Gulf plain by the Zagros Mountains. However, the province of Khuzestan—a flat lowland plain—lies west of the mountains at the northern end of the Gulf. Most of its population is Arab, and in fact it used to be known as Arabistan. But Iran annexed the territory early in the 20th century. Some Arabs, including various Iraqi governments, refused to recognize the loss of Arabistan.

The Shatt al Arab—the waterway formed by the merging of Iraq's two major rivers, the Tigris and the Euphrates—provides the only access for ships to the main Iraqi port of Basra and the big Iranian port at Khorramshahr. Major oil fields in both countries border the Shatt, and oil is exported from terminals along the river. Iran and Iraq have long squabbled over the waterway.

A 1937 treaty gave Iraq control of most of the Shatt, spurring considerable Iranian resentment. In 1969 the shah decided to ignore the treaty and use his navy to escort Iranian ships. The tense situation continued until 1975, when Iran and Iraq signed a new agreement in Algeria giving both countries equal rights in the waterway. Yet other border disputes involving smaller areas in the mountainous region to the north remained unresolved.

Iran-Iraq relations were complicated as well by the Kurdish question. The Kurds are Sunni Muslims but form a distinct ethnic or national group separate from Persians, Arabs, or Turks. Their ancestral lands extend over parts of Turkey, Syria, Iraq, Iran, and Armenia. From the early 20th century the Kurds sought an independent state of their own, but this goal was thwarted, first by the European powers and then by the governments of the region. In the 1960s the Kurds of northern Iraq rebelled, and the shah of Iran aided their cause as a way of pressuring the Baghdad regime. Iran's promise to stop supporting the Kurdish rebels in Iraq was a major reason why Iraq signed the 1975 agreement on the Shatt al Arab.

The Road to War

At the end of the 1970s the troubled relationship between Iran and Iraq became even more volatile, largely as the result of two developments. The first was the Islamic Revolution—or, more precisely, the desire of Iran's new religious leaders to export the revolution. Though they held a dim view of the governments of many Muslim countries, the Iranian mullahs were especially hostile toward the regime in Baghdad. They reviled the Iraqi government not only for its strongly secular orientation but also for its repression of Iraq's Shia majority. Iran began funding underground Shia opposition groups, one of which attempted to assassinate Iraq's foreign minister.

The second ominous development in the Gulf at the end of the 1970s was Saddam Hussein's seizure of power in Iraq. Since 1968, after a coup installed his cousin General Ahmad Hasan al-Bakr at the head of a Baathist government, Saddam had served as Iraq's vice president. Behind the scenes, he methodically brought the levers of power under his own control. In 1979 Saddam eased al-Bakr aside, made himself president, and on July 16 orchestrated a ruthless purge of Baath Party rivals.

Saddam was now Iraq's unquestioned leader. But his ambitions were not limited to Iraq. He wanted to be recognized as the leading figure in the entire Arab world.

Saddam could not countenance Iran's efforts to foment Shia opposition to his regime, and he also railed against the supposed unfairness of the 1975 Shatt al Arab agreement. But, equally important, he saw Iran as a target of opportunity. He calculated that Iran was still weakened by the chaos that had accompanied the Islamic Revolution, and that its leaders were distracted by the standoff with the United States over the American hostages. He also believed that Iran's non-Persian population had little allegiance to the Shia mullahs ruling Iran. In particular, Saddam believed that the largely Arab

General Ahmad Hasan al-Bakr (right) became president of Iraq after a 1968 coup. But by 1976, when this photo was taken, Vice President Saddam Hussein (left) was well on his way to consolidating power in his own hands. In 1979 Saddam obliged al-Bakr, his uncle, to retire and made himself president.

population of Iran's Khuzestan Province, just across the Shatt al Arab from Iraq, would eagerly rise up against the Tehran government and ask to be reunited with Iraq in the event of an Iraqi invasion.

Besides being close to Iraq and having a sizable Arab population, Khuzestan offered other advantages as the site of an Iraqi military strike. It contained most of Iran's oil, the loss of which would cripple Iran economically. Khuzestan's terrain—low, flat, and with few natural obstacles—was also favorable to an invading army.

Iraq Attacks

On September 17, 1980, after weeks of increasing tensions between Iran and Iraq, Saddam renounced the Shatt al Arab treaty. Five days later Iraqi warplanes bombed Iranian air bases as Iraqi army units stormed across the border into Iran. Saddam's forces quickly drove deep into Khuzestan Province,

Smiling Iraqi soldiers mock an image of Ayatollah Khomeini, September 1980. Iraq seemed headed for a quick victory in the first weeks after its invasion of Iran. In fact, eight years of pitiless fighting would ensue.

even reaching the base of the Zagros Mountains. By November the Iraqis had taken some 4,000 square miles (10,360 sq km) of Iranian territory and controlled the major port of Khorramshahr.

Iraq's early success, however, was not as secure as it seemed. The initial bombing campaign had failed to cripple the Iranian air force, which struck back. Iraqi units were repulsed at the strategic town of Abadan, and pockets of Iranian soldiers remained entrenched behind the Iraqi front. Furthermore, Saddam's prediction that the Arabs of Khuzestan would rally to his side proved incorrect. By the end of 1980 the Iraqi invasion had stalled.

Both sides tried to enlist external support. Saddam claimed his forces were protecting the Arab world against Iranian aggression. He pressured the other Arab Gulf states to loan Iraq large sums of money for arms and equipment.

Not all Arab states backed Iraq, however. Syria, for example, allied itself with Tehran because of its long and sometimes violent rivalry with Iraq.

Stalemate

Gradually Iran gained the initiative. Its Revolutionary Guards—originally established to protect the Islamic Revolution from internal threats—fought fanatically. In addition, Iran, with its much larger population, enjoyed a huge manpower advantage over Iraq. Tens of thousands of volunteers, many of them too young or too old to serve in the regular army, were recruited for special militia units that carried out "human wave" assaults against Iraqi positions.

By June 1982, with Iranian forces gaining steadily, Saddam Hussein signaled his willingness to withdraw his troops from Iranian territory and negotiate a settlement to the war. The offer was rebuffed. In the early weeks of the fighting, when Iraq appeared to be winning, Ayatollah Khomeini had said that the war would not end until "the government of heathens in Baghdad topples." Now that the advantage had shifted to the Iranian side, Tehran had even less inclination to negotiate with Saddam.

In July, for the first time since the outbreak of the conflict, Iranian units launched an offensive on Iraqi soil. The target was the strategic southern city of Basra, and the main tactic was the human-wave assault. The ill-trained and badly equipped volunteers, some of them as young as nine years old, were slaughtered by the thousands before the Iranian offensive petered out.

Similarly, the Iraqis repulsed a series of Iranian offensives the following year, with both sides sustaining appallingly high casualties. For many military observers, the fighting in the Iran-Iraq War was reminiscent of a conflict that had been waged seven decades earlier: World War I. The Iranian and Iraqi sides hunkered down in defensive trenches, exchanged heavy artillery fire, and periodically launched massive infantry assaults that accomplished little but cost huge numbers of lives. Iraq also employed a weapon first developed in World War I and subsequently banned by the international community for its horrific effects: poison gas.

From the early part of the war, both countries had sought to hurt their enemy's economy, in part by targeting oil production facilities and ports. In early 1984, however, Iraq raised the stakes with the large-scale targeting of ships—including the commercial vessels of neutral countries—calling at Iranian ports as far south as Bushehr in the Persian Gulf. Iran soon responded by attacking Kuwaiti and Saudi oil tankers that were well outside the war zone, sending the message that the Gulf Arab states would pay a price if Iraq continued to try to strangle shipping to and from Iran.

For the industrialized countries, including the United States, the escalation of the so-called tanker war was an alarming development. Much of the world's oil supply traveled through the Gulf, and the Iran-Iraq conflict threatened to slow that supply to a trickle. Iranian leaders even intimated that they might choke off all maritime traffic through the Gulf at the narrow Strait of Hormuz, but—most likely because this would hurt their country's economy as much as Iraq's—never followed through.

In the face of continuing attacks on commercial shipping, however, the U.S. Navy began escorting oil tankers through the Gulf. In 1987, responding to requests from the government of Kuwait, U.S. leaders even agreed to have 11 Kuwaiti tankers "reflagged" as American vessels. This effectively deterred direct Iranian attacks, though Iran did continue to lay mines in the Gulf, taking a toll on commercial ships and several U.S. naval vessels. After an Iranian mine severely damaged the American frigate *Samuel B. Roberts* in April 1988, the United States retaliated heavily, destroying three Iranian warships and a half-dozen smaller vessels, in addition to several oil platforms.

Officially, the United States remained neutral during the Iran-Iraq War. However, from about 1982 U.S. policy tilted toward Iraq. Directly or indirectly, the United States provided Saddam Hussein with financial and technical assistance, intelligence, and limited military equipment—though American officials had no intention of giving Saddam a decisive advantage. (He was, after all, a sworn enemy of the closest U.S. ally in the Middle East, Israel.)

America's Cold War nemesis, the Soviet Union, also was neutral at the outset of the Iran-Iraq War, refusing to sell arms to either party in the conflict. However, fearing the consequences of an Iranian victory, Soviet leaders eventually decided to supply Iraq with massive amounts of sophisticated military equipment.

Iran, meanwhile, faced a U.S. and international boycott that prevented it from obtaining replacements and spare parts for the largely American-made weapons systems the shah had purchased. (In a notorious breach of the American arms embargo, officials in the administration of President Ronald Reagan secretly provided Iran with antitank and antiaircraft missiles in 1985 and 1986, hoping that Iran would in turn pressure a terrorist group it sponsored to release American hostages being held in Lebanon. But those shipments were halted after the details came to light in what became known as the Iran-contra scandal.)

Iran's shortage of military equipment was becoming increasingly severe in early 1988, as the war entered another horrifying phase: the so-called war of the cities. For more than six weeks beginning in late February, Iran and Iraq fired missiles at each other's major population centers, including their respective capitals. Finally, on July 18, 1988, Ayatollah Khomeini reversed course and accepted a United Nations–brokered cease-fire, which took effect one month later.

Ramifications

After eight years the guns had finally fallen silent. But the cease-fire left contentious issues unresolved. These included the question of blame, the

Journalists document the aftermath of the March 1988 chemical-weapons attack on the Kurdish village of Halabja, in northern Iraq. About 5,000 civilians were killed in the atrocity, which was ordered by Saddam Hussein to punish Kurds for sympathizing with Iran during the Iran-Iraq War.

exchange of prisoners, Iran's demand for compensation, even the status of the Shatt al Arab (Saddam would be forced to accept a return to the 1975 agreement only after embroiling his country in another war).

The scope of the carnage and destruction, however, was all too apparent. Combined casualties for the two sides had probably exceeded 1 million—and they may have been double that. Economic costs were also severe. Billions of dollars had been diverted from development projects to fund the war efforts, and extensive damage to oil installations cost both countries billions more in potential oil revenues, during the conflict and in its aftermath.

Another consequence of the war was a heightened awareness of the vulnerability of the Persian Gulf oil supply, along with increased American involvement in Gulf security. The U.S. Navy had augmented its presence in and around the Gulf, and American officials made arrangements to stockpile arms and equipment in the Arab Gulf states in case of a future crisis.

The Iran-Iraq War also had the effect of bringing the Arab Gulf states of Saudi Arabia, Kuwait, Bahrain, Qatar, the United Arab Emirates, and Oman closer together. These smaller states, all of them conservative monarchies aligned with the West, had long been wary of intrigues against them by Saddam Hussein's Iraq. At the same time, however, they were suspicious of the shah's massive military buildup, and Iran seemed even more menacing after the Shia mullahs came to power.

In May 1981, with the Iran-Iraq War raging, the six other Gulf states formed an organization devoted to mutual security and economic integration, called the Gulf Cooperation Council (GCC). A secretariat was created in Riyadh, Saudi Arabia, and the leaders of the member states agreed to meet annually at a summit.

Over the years, the GCC countries made considerable progress on economic cooperation. For example, they created common standards for food and industrial products and abolished internal barriers to trade, travel, and investment. Progress on security matters, however, proved more difficult. The GCC countries shared the goal of reducing their dependence on the

A meeting of the Gulf Cooperation Council. Comprising Saudi Arabia, Kuwait, Bahrain, Qatar, the United Arab Emirates, and Oman, the GCC was formed in May 1981 to promote the mutual security and economic integration of the Gulf's smaller nations.

United States for protection, but they disagreed on how to accomplish that. In 1984 a small GCC defense force, known as Peninsula Shield, was established, primarily on the initiative of Saudi Arabia. However, that force's shortcomings would be clearly exposed in 1990, when Saddam Hussein's hostile attentions turned to an Arab neighbor.

(Right) U.S. president George H. W. Bush answers a question at an August 8, 1990, press conference. Earlier that day, Bush had announced the deployment of American troops to Saudi Arabia, to deter a possible Iraqi invasion. (Opposite) As Iraqi troops retreated from Kuwait during the 1991 Gulf War, they set fire to oil wells, creating an ecological disaster.

4 *Iraq's Invasion of Kuwait and The Gulf War*

*J*n September 1980, when he ordered the invasion of Iran, Saddam Hussein had expected a quick victory. That had proved to be a monumental miscalculation. After eight years of horrific fighting, Iraq had achieved nothing, and in the opinion of many military analysts, only international help had enabled Saddam to avert a decisive defeat at the hands of the Iranians.

Yet Saddam saw matters differently. In his view, the long and costly stalemate actually represented a victory. Iraq had fought its larger neighbor to a draw, and Saddam remained firmly in charge in Baghdad despite Ayatollah Khomeini's promise to topple his regime. Moreover, Saddam believed that many Arabs now saw him as the true leader of the Arab world because he had stood up to the Iranians.

Saddam's assessment may have been distorted, but in certain respects the war with Iran had indeed strengthened his hand. Whereas Tehran was now more isolated internationally, Baghdad had seen relations with the West improve. In return for their wartime assistance, Western countries had received Iraqi military and development contracts. The United States, which continued to view Iran as an enemy, had reestablished diplomatic relations with Iraq (official ties had been cut off as a result of the 1967 Six-Day War between Israel and Arab countries). While the U.S. State Department publicly condemned Iraq's use of chemical weapons—against Iranian soldiers and, in 1988, against Iraqi Kurd civilians in the village of Halabja—the administrations of President Reagan and his successor, President George H. W. Bush, failed to materially punish this violation of the Geneva Conventions.

Despite Saddam's diplomatic gains, there was no denying that the war with Iran had left Iraq in dire economic straits. Estimated rebuilding costs totaled some $225 billion. In addition, Iraq owed more than $75 billion to foreign creditors, most of this sum to the states of the Gulf Cooperation Council, which had loaned their Arab neighbor large amounts of money to fund its war effort.

Iraq's prospects for economic recovery hinged on revenue from oil sales, and the country's damaged infrastructure was only one impediment. In 1988 the price of crude oil was low—slightly more than $15 per barrel, or less than half the price in 1980, at the beginning of the Iran-Iraq War. The low prices dramatically limited Iraq's potential earnings—according to the country's oil minister, each dollar less per barrel translated into $1 billion in lost annual revenues.

Many factors had contributed to a glut of oil on the market, and thus to the depressed prices. But two Gulf states—Kuwait and the United Arab Emirates—were worsening the situation by exceeding the production quotas set for them by the Organization of Petroleum Exporting Countries (OPEC). With 11 member countries possessing a combined three-quarters of the world's proven petroleum reserves, OPEC could significantly influence the global supply—and hence the price—of crude oil if its members respected the limits the organization placed on the amount of oil they were allowed to pump.

In December 1988 Iraq—a founding member of OPEC—appealed to the organization to raise its production quota so that it could earn more revenue for reconstruction. OPEC agreed to only a slight production increase for Iraq, and it failed to take meaningful action on another Iraqi request: that the quotas of other member countries be enforced. To Saddam's increasing resentment, Kuwait and the UAE continued to pump more oil than their OPEC quota allowed.

Saddam also fumed at the GCC states as a whole. He argued that the Iraqi nation had sacrificed much to defend them from Iran, and they should show their gratitude by canceling Iraq's war debts. This suggestion fell on deaf ears, however.

Over the next couple years, Saddam continued to rail against all of the Arab Gulf states, but he reserved special contempt for Kuwait. Border disputes had long been a source of friction between the two countries. In addition, Kuwait repeatedly refused Iraqi requests to cede or lease two islands strategically located near Umm Qasr, Iraq's only port not on the Shatt al Arab.

"A Poisoned Dagger"

By July 1990 Iraq's relations with the Gulf states, and especially Kuwait, had become even more antagonistic. Kuwait was demanding the repayment of its war loans to Iraq. In turn, Iraq accused Kuwait of stealing its oil by "slant drilling" under the border to reach the Iraqi part of the massive Rumaila oil field. Further, Saddam Hussein threatened to take military action against any OPEC member, including Kuwait, that persisted in pumping more oil than its quota. In a televised speech he delivered on July 17, Saddam charged that Kuwait, along with the United Arab Emirates, had "stabbed Iraq in the back with a poisoned dagger." On the 18th, some 30,000 Iraqi soldiers were transported to the border with Kuwait. In the coming days, many more would follow.

Alarmed by his neighbor's increasingly aggressive posture, the ruler of Kuwait, Emir Jabir al-Ahmad al-Sabah, appealed for help in defusing the situation. Egyptian president Hosni Mubarak offered to mediate. On July 25 Mubarak met with Saddam Hussein, who pledged to try to resolve his differences with Kuwait peacefully. The Egyptians set about arranging a conference.

In July 1990, as the anti-Kuwait rhetoric of Saddam Hussein (left) grew increasingly bellicose, Egyptian president Hosni Mubarak (right) attempted to mediate. Mubarak's efforts ultimately proved fruitless.

Shortly after his meeting with Mubarak, Saddam called in the U.S. ambassador to Iraq, April Glaspie, and asked about the U.S. opinion on Iraq's dispute with Kuwait. Ambassador Glaspie informed him that the United States did not take sides in Arab-Arab disputes. Later, some critics would claim that this conversation essentially gave Saddam a "green light" to invade Kuwait. But Glaspie was simply repeating U.S. policy, and Saddam may already have made up his mind on that course of action.

On July 31, representatives of Iraq and Kuwait gathered in Jidda, Saudi Arabia, to discuss their differences. But the talks collapsed the following day.

Invasion and Response

Beginning at 2 A.M. on August 2, more than 100,000 Iraqi soldiers, backed by hundreds of tanks, stormed across the border into Kuwait. Despite the weeks of deepening tensions with Iraq, the invasion caught Kuwait's armed forces by surprise. Only one unit offered meaningful resistance; the rest retreated. Within hours Saddam's army controlled all of Kuwait.

The emir and other members of Kuwait's ruling Al-Sabah family escaped to Saudi Arabia, where they would set up a government-in-exile. Tens of thousands of ordinary Kuwaitis, as well as guest workers, also fled the country.

Only hours after Saddam's forces had swept across the border, television and radio broadcasts in Iraq and Kuwait announced that the Iraqis had been invited into Kuwait by a Kuwaiti revolutionary group that had overthrown the corrupt and autocratic regime of the emir and would ultimately hold "free, honest elections." But the ruse fooled no one, and from around the world the invasion was greeted with public condemnation. Margaret Thatcher, the British prime minister, called Iraq's actions "absolutely unacceptable." President George H. W. Bush characterized the invasion as a "naked act of aggression" and warned that the United States would consider all options in dealing with Iraq. Meeting in emergency session, the United Nations Security Council denounced the invasion and demanded that Iraq immediately and unconditionally withdraw from Kuwait.

Three days later President Bush promised that Iraq's conquest would not stand. But in the short term at least, the United States could do little to force the Iraqis out of Kuwait. Nor was the fate of Kuwait the Bush administration's only concern. Saddam had the world's fourth-largest army, and given the easy success of his move against Kuwait, he might be tempted to risk an invasion of Iraq's other southern neighbor, Saudi Arabia. An Iraqi conquest of Saudi Arabia would give Saddam a stranglehold on Persian Gulf oil production, with potentially disastrous consequences for the industrialized economies of Japan, Western Europe, and the United States.

On August 6, the same day the United Nations Security Council voted unanimously to impose an economic embargo on Iraq, a delegation of U.S. officials led by Secretary of Defense Dick Cheney met with the Saudi ruler, King Fahd. Cheney warned the king that Iraqi troops were massed along Saudi Arabia's northern border. He requested permission to deploy American military forces to Saudi Arabia to prevent a possible Iraqi invasion. King Fahd agreed. Soon after, elements of the 82nd Airborne Division arrived in Saudi Arabia, the vanguard in what would become a massive military buildup code-named Operation Desert Shield.

On August 8 Iraq announced the annexation of Kuwait. President Bush, meanwhile, delivered a nationally televised speech to the American people in which he set forth four key goals of U.S. policy: withdrawal of Iraqi forces from Kuwait; restoration of the legitimate government of Kuwait; peace and stability in the Persian Gulf; and protection of

U.S. Marines begin setting up a defensive position in northern Saudi Arabia during Operation Desert Shield.

American lives (some 3,000 U.S. citizens remained trapped in Iraqi-occupied Kuwait).

Two days later Saddam called for a jihad, or holy war, against the United States and Israel. Soon afterward, he offered to withdraw from Kuwait if certain conditions were met, including an Israeli withdrawal from the Palestinian territory it had occupied since 1967. These attempts to link Israel and the Palestinian issue with the situation in the Gulf were obviously calculated to drum up support for Iraq among Arabs.

Throughout the unfolding Gulf crisis Saddam's actions did win some support from fellow Arabs, but overall the Arab world was divided. Many ordinary people, particularly in the poorer Arab countries, had little sympathy for Kuwait (or, for that matter, for the other rich oil-producing Gulf states). Kuwaitis were resented for their wealth, their perceived indifference to the plight of Arabs in other countries, and their treatment of Arab guest workers inside Kuwait. Pro-Iraq demonstrations were held in the capitals of many Arab countries. At the same time, however, most Arab governments did not support Saddam. In fact, the 21-member League of Arab States voted on August 10 to contribute troops to help protect Saudi Arabia—though Iraq, Libya, and the Palestine Liberation Organization (PLO) were opposed and several other Arab League members abstained from the vote.

Building the Coalition

The military contributions of Arab states had great political significance in the multinational effort to roll back Iraqi aggression in Kuwait. Almost immediately after the invasion, the Bush administration had begun consulting key allies, and even traditional adversaries such as the Soviet Union, in an effort to build international consensus on restoring the sovereignty of Kuwait. Even though the Cold War was essentially over (the Soviet Union would collapse completely in 1991) and the United States was now the world's lone superpower, President Bush shied away from unilateral U.S. action. In the "new world order" he envisioned, the United States might exercise a leadership role, but breaches of international law would be met with a unified international response based on the principles of—and ideally sanctioned by—the United Nations. More than 30 countries eventually joined the U.S.-led coalition opposing Iraq.

As the Desert Shield military buildup proceeded in Saudi Arabia, Iraq transported additional units into Kuwait. It also began moving Western hostages to critical installations. These "human shields," the Iraqis hoped, would deter aerial bombing by the United States and its allies. Meanwhile, reports of Iraqi atrocities trickled out of Kuwait. In strengthening their hold in the face of an underground resistance movement, the Iraqis were evidently making use of arbitrary arrests, torture, and summary executions.

Negotiations and Diplomacy

On August 28 Saddam's regime declared that Kuwait was Iraq's "19th province." The basis of this claim was that because the territory of Kuwait had been administratively linked with the Basra province of Mesopotamia during the Ottoman period, it rightfully belonged now to Iraq. But twice before—in 1932 and 1963—Iraqi leaders had signed border agreements recognizing Kuwaiti sovereignty.

Given Saddam's claims that Kuwait belonged to Iraq, and the U.S. insistence that the pre-invasion government of Kuwait be restored after a full Iraqi withdrawal, the two sides appeared to have little to discuss. Nevertheless, efforts to resolve the situation through negotiation and diplomacy continued. Iraq floated a number of proposals after the rejection of its August 12 offer to withdraw from Kuwait if Israel withdrew from occupied territories. One Iraqi proposal offered a withdrawal from Kuwait and the release of all Western hostages in exchange for the lifting of the UN's economic embargo and a guarantee that Iraq would receive the Kuwaiti-owned islands near Umm Qasr. As with other Iraqi offers, these conditions were rejected. Jordan and Libya separately proposed unsuccessful peace plans, both of which were widely viewed to favor Iraq—much to the resentment of the Kuwaiti and Saudi governments. UN Secretary-General Javier Pérez de Cuellar held fruitless talks with Iraqi representatives in Jordan. Saddam unsuccessfully sought to persuade Iraq's longtime ally, the Soviet Union, to support him and rebuffed a succession of Soviet plans to resolve the Kuwait issue peacefully. Later peace plans proposed by Morocco and France failed as well.

Preparing for a Fight

By the end of October, U.S. military leaders were confident that they had sufficient forces in place to repel an Iraqi invasion of Saudi Arabia. But expelling Iraq from Kuwait by force would require more troops. In early November, President Bush announced that he was ordering the deployment of additional units to the Gulf. Over the next weeks, total U.S. troop levels went from 230,000 to about half a million. They were supported by some 2,000 tanks and 1,800 combat aircraft, in addition to more than 100 ships. U.S. forces were augmented by sizable contingents from other nations, including European countries such as Great Britain and France, and Arab countries such as Saudi Arabia, Egypt, and Syria. Canada, Italy, and South Korea sent combat aircraft. Naval combat and support ships came from Portugal, Australia, Belgium, the Netherlands, Spain, and Greece. Pakistan, Bangladesh, Senegal, and Niger sent smaller contingents of soldiers, while

Czechoslovakia, New Zealand, and Poland were among the countries providing medical assistance.

Many countries helped finance the coalition's military effort in the Gulf. Out of a total of $54 billion pledged, $11 billion came from Japan, $8 billion from Germany, and $16 billion from Saudi Arabia and Kuwait.

On November 29 the UN Security Council passed Resolution 678. It provided Iraq "one final opportunity" to comply with previous United Nations resolutions on Kuwait. It also established a deadline—January 15, 1991—for the withdrawal of Iraqi forces from Kuwait. After that date, the U.S.-led coalition was authorized "to use all necessary means" to expel the Iraqis.

By December 1990 all the Western hostages being held by Iraq were released, but Saddam Hussein made no move to pull his troops out of Kuwait. As the UN-established deadline approached, diplomatic efforts to avert a war continued. Talks in Geneva, Switzerland, between Iraq's foreign minister and the U.S. secretary of state collapsed on January 9. The personal envoy of Soviet leader Mikhail Gorbachev tried frantically to persuade Saddam to withdraw from Kuwait, but the Iraqi dictator appeared convinced that the 35-nation coalition arrayed against him would not attack.

Operation Desert Storm: The Air Campaign

The UN's January 15 deadline passed with no Iraqi withdrawal and no coalition attack. At about 3:00 A.M. on the 17th, however, residents of Baghdad awoke to a cacophony of explosions and antiaircraft fire. Operation Desert Storm, the coalition military campaign to liberate Kuwait, had begun.

War in Kuwait seemed inevitable when the *Arab News*, an English-language newspaper in Saudi Arabia, went to press on January 11, 1991. The UN deadline for Iraq's complete withdrawal from Kuwait was just four days away.

The initial phase of Operation Desert Storm consisted of an intensive aerial bombing campaign designed to destroy Iraqi air defenses, command-and-control capabilities, weapons research and production facilities (of particular concern were Iraq's chemical and nuclear weapons programs), and critical infrastructure such as bridges and power plants. The coalition brought an enormous amount of firepower to bear, dropping tens of thousands of tons of bombs and launching hundreds of cruise missiles—a weapon never before used in war—from ships in the Persian Gulf.

Iraq's defenses proved no match for U.S. and coalition airpower. In fact, during the entire Gulf War, coalition aircraft would fly more than 116,000 combat sorties (individual missions) but lose just 42 aircraft in combat. The few Iraqi pilots who ventured into the skies to engage their coalition counterparts met a swift end. Saddam—seeking to preserve his air force for future use—devised a novel strategy: he had more than 135 Iraqi warplanes flown to Iran to prevent their destruction. Unfortunately for Saddam, Iranian officials decided to incorporate some of the planes of their longtime enemy into Iran's air force.

If Iraq could not fight an air war on equal terms with the coalition, it was not entirely without options. It had hundreds of Scud missiles. Though not especially accurate, the Scuds were easily concealed and could be fired from mobile launchers that were hard to find and destroy from the air. Within a day of the first coalition air strikes, the Iraqis began launching Scud missiles into Israel. The clear purpose was to provoke Israeli retaliation and thereby to produce a rift among the coalition's Arab members. However, the United States rushed Patriot antimissile batteries to Israel and convinced Israeli officials to stay out of the conflict.

Iraq also attempted to pressure the coalition into halting its campaign by creating an environmental disaster. By the last week in January, Iraqi forces had begun blowing up Kuwaiti oil wells and dumping oil into the Gulf.

On January 30, Iraqi forces drove south out of Kuwait and captured the town of al-Khafji, Saudi Arabia, killing a dozen U.S. Marines in ferocious fighting. Coalition troops quickly retook the town, however, and for the most part Iraqi forces remained entrenched in positions in the deserts of southern Kuwait and Iraq. In the event of a ground campaign, Iraqi commanders anticipated the kind of fighting they had seen during the war with Iran, and they believed they could inflict heavy casualties and gain a stalemate when coalition forces launched frontal assaults against their fortified positions.

As the coalition air campaign continued to pound targets in Iraq and Iraqi units inside Kuwait, Soviet leader Mikhail Gorbachev frantically searched for a way to avoid a full-scale ground war. In mid-February, Gorbachev dispatched an envoy to Baghdad, and soon Baghdad announced its willingness to withdraw from Kuwait. The Soviet ambassador to the United Nations said that his country "accepted with hope" that message, though he conceded that some details would have to be worked out. But the coalition countries were nearly unanimous in dismissing Baghdad's withdrawal offer out of hand, primarily because the Iraqis wanted to link it to a pullback of all coalition forces from the Gulf, an Israeli withdrawal from Palestinian lands, and other unacceptable conditions. President Bush quickly branded the Iraqi peace offer "a cruel hoax" and reiterated the coalition's insistence that Iraq leave Kuwait unconditionally. "But there is another way for the bloodshed to stop," Bush declared, "and that is for the Iraqi military and the Iraqi people to take matters into their own hands, to force Saddam Hussein, the dictator, to step aside and to comply with the UN resolutions." This apparent expansion of the coalition's objectives to include the overthrow of Saddam would have fateful consequences.

Meanwhile, Mikhail Gorbachev continued to search for a peace formula acceptable to both Iraq and the coalition in talks with the Iraqi foreign minister, Tariq Aziz. On February 22 Moscow announced that Saddam had accepted Gorbachev's latest proposal and would withdraw from Kuwait. However, while the Iraqi dictator had dropped some of the conditions he insisted on earlier, he still refused to pay reparations to Kuwait or even formally recognize its independence, as UN resolutions required. Nevertheless, Gorbachev, in a phone call to George Bush, personally implored the president to use this latest opening as an opportunity for further negotiations. Bush refused, instead issuing an ultimatum: unless Iraq withdrew from Kuwait within 24 hours, the coalition would launch a ground offensive.

Ground War

Bush's deadline passed with no Iraqi withdrawal. In the early morning hours of February 24, the coalition's long-anticipated ground offensive began.

Over the previous months, approximately 680,000 coalition troops—about three-quarters of them American—had assembled in the region. Opposing them were several hundred thousand Iraqi soldiers stationed in southern Iraq and Kuwait; many Iraqis had already deserted.

Iraq's generals were expecting two coalition thrusts: first, a frontal assault into southern Kuwait, and second—thanks to a coalition deception effort—an amphibious landing along Kuwait's Gulf coast. They deployed their forces accordingly.

The coalition, under the military leadership of American general Norman Schwarzkopf, had actually planned a three-pronged attack. One prong—consisting of two U.S. Marine divisions flanked by two armies composed of Arab troops—would indeed punch into southern Kuwait. This, Schwarzkopf believed, would cause elite Republican Guard units being held in reserve in Iraq to move south and enter the fight. In the second prong U.S. airborne divisions, along with an American infantry division and a French light armored division, would drive into Iraq several hundred miles to the west and sweep toward Kuwait's northern border. This would cut the supply lines, and the escape routes, of Iraqi forces in Kuwait. The third prong—dubbed the "left hook" and consisting of U.S. heavy armor, armored cavalry, and infantry divisions, along with a British armored division—would then race through the desert to engage the Republican Guard divisions that had moved south. Trapped, the Republican Guard—the backbone of Saddam's army and the foundation of his power—would be annihilated.

From the early hours of the ground campaign, the fighting was entirely one-sided. During the initial attack into Kuwait, the Marines quickly broke through Iraqi defenses. The front-line Iraqi troops were largely conscripts, men drafted into the army. Many had fought in the long war with Iran, and they had just been pounded relentlessly from the air for more than a month. Their morale was low.

"We expected casualties somewhere in the 25 to 30 percent range," Marine colonel John Admire recalled. "But there were essentially no firefights, essentially no battles. The Iraqis were there, but they chose . . . not to fight. In many respects, they could retreat and they could surrender much faster than we could attack or advance and . . . the war really became a war

After nearly six weeks of aerial bombing, the coalition ground campaign against Iraq finally began on February 24, 1991. Here American M-1A1 Abrams tanks race through the desert of southern Iraq.

of collection of enemy prisoners of war." In the first hours of the Marine advance, an estimated 8,000 Iraqis surrendered.

On February 25, the second day of the Desert Storm ground campaign, Iraqi armored units mounted a massive counterattack in Kuwait, but they were quickly smashed. The way to Kuwait City was now open for coalition forces, and Iraqi soldiers who had occupied the capital for seven months began a panicked retreat toward Iraq in whatever vehicles they could get their hands on. Coalition warplanes bombed the long convoy on the main highway heading north, killing thousands. Elsewhere, Iraqi soldiers set Kuwait's oil wells on fire as they retreated; the fires would take months to put out and resulted in an ecological disaster.

Early on the morning of February 27, coalition forces entered Kuwait City to a tumultuous welcome. Saddam, meanwhile, announced that Iraqi forces had withdrawn completely from Kuwait.

The coalition's liberation of Kuwait had been unexpectedly easy and rapid, outstripping General Schwarzkopf's plans for the decisive "left hook" maneuver. The Republican Guard divisions had not moved south into Kuwait to counter the initial Marine attack, and thus they were not completely surrounded as Schwarzkopf had envisioned. On the afternoon of February 26, the leading elements of the coalition left hook, racing eastward through the desert of Iraq, had first encountered Republican Guard units. By the morning of the 27th, as coalition units rolled into Kuwait City, the bulk of a Republican Guard division had already been destroyed in the desert. Within hours the remaining five Republican Guard divisions were trapped, and Schwarzkopf believed that with one more day his forces could annihilate them.

Cease-fire

However, in Washington, D.C., President Bush and his advisers decided to call an end to the fighting. "Kuwait is liberated. Iraq's army is defeated," Bush

Coalition soldiers and Kuwaiti civilians celebrate the liberation of Kuwait City, February 27, 1991.

declared in a televised address. "Our military objectives are met. I am pleased to announce that at midnight tonight, Eastern Standard Time, exactly 100 hours since ground operations commenced and six weeks since the start of Operation Desert Storm, all United States and coalition forces will suspend offensive combat operations." Three hours later, at 8 A.M. local time, the cease-fire went into effect in Iraq.

The Gulf War had been one of history's most lopsided conflicts. The coalition had suffered only 240 battle deaths (148 of them were Americans). Initial estimates put the number of Iraqi soldiers killed at 100,000 or more, but many military historians came to believe that figure was too high. Even if later estimates of 25,000 to 40,000 are closer to the mark, the coalition's victory was nothing short of stunning, particularly considering that more than 70,000 Iraqi soldiers surrendered or were captured as well.

The Republican Guard, without which Saddam Hussein could not maintain his power, had been badly mauled. About one-third had been killed, and the survivors lost half their equipment in the fight with, and retreat from, coalition forces.

"[Neither] the president nor any of us thought at that time," U.S. secretary of state James Baker recalled, "that Saddam would . . . continue in power having suffered such a . . . resounding defeat." They were wrong.

The Gulf War reduced Saddam Hussein's capacity to menace his neighbors, but not to repress his own people. (Opposite) Displaced Kurds seek refuge from the Iraqi army's brutal offensive near the border with Turkey. (Right) UN inspectors examine a container of nerve agent. Weapons inspections, a condition of the Gulf War cease-fire, eventually eliminated Iraq's chemical, biological, and nuclear weapons programs.

5 *Unresolved Tensions*

$\mathcal{T}$he momentous events that shook the Persian Gulf during the period 1978–1991 would continue to reverberate in the years that followed. Major sources of tension within the Gulf, and between Gulf states and the rest of the world, were still unresolved. Security in the region remained elusive.

The Shia and Kurdish Uprisings

Even the Gulf War, which initially seemed like an unqualified success for the United States and the international coalition it had assembled, would come to be regarded as an incomplete victory. Saddam Hussein managed to retain power, and though he had led his country into another disastrous conflict, he considered himself a hero for having stood up to the greatest assembly of armed forces in the history of the world. In the wake of this "triumph," he would brutally strengthen his hold on Iraq, continue to menace Gulf neighbors, and thoroughly vex the international community.

During the first days of March 1991, a spontaneous and disorganized uprising broke out among the Shia of southern Iraq. Again, President Bush urged the Iraqi people to take matters into their own hands and overthrow Saddam.

Meanwhile, General Norman Schwarzkopf and other coalition commanders were meeting their Iraqi counterparts near the town of Safwan, Iraq, to work out terms for a permanent cease-fire. Among other conditions, the Iraqis agreed to release all coalition prisoners of war and imprisoned Kuwaitis, renounce any future claims to Kuwait, and pay compensation for damages caused by the invasion. A temporary cease-fire line was established, and it was agreed that coalition forces would remain on occupied territory in southern Iraq until a permanent cease-fire went into effect. In the meantime, to prevent potential threats to coalition forces, Iraqis were forbidden to fly fixed-wing aircraft. However, when Saddam's generals asked Schwarzkopf whether Iraq would be permitted to fly helicopters, he consented. It did not seem a particularly significant matter. In fact, the consequences of Schwarzkopf's decision would be enormous.

Using transport helicopters, Saddam quickly moved loyal army units south. Helicopter gunships backed the infantry soldiers as they battled the Shia rebels. Some of the fighting occurred within sight of American soldiers near the cease-fire line, but—despite President Bush's verbal encouragement of the uprising—the American forces had orders not to intervene. Within weeks thousands of Shia had been killed and the rebellion crushed.

Meanwhile, Kurds in northern Iraq—also inspired by the American president—had launched their own uprising. With political leaders and militias, the Kurds were more organized than the Shia. But in early April, after suppressing the Shia rebellion, Saddam's army unleashed a furious campaign against the Kurds, whose militias were soon overwhelmed. President Bush made it clear that the United States would not intervene in support of the rebels. "I do not want to push American forces beyond our mandate," he announced on April 3. "We've done the heavy lifting."

That same day, the United Nations Security Council passed Resolution 687, which set the terms of the Gulf War's formal cease-fire. In addition to the conditions earlier agreed to, Resolution 687 required that Iraq abandon its programs to produce chemical, biological, and nuclear weapons, and that Iraq destroy any stockpiles of these weapons of mass destruction (WMD) it had amassed. Until Iraq had complied fully, strict economic sanctions would be kept in place. On April 6, Iraq officially accepted the terms, and the permanent cease-fire went into effect five days later.

Peace had by no means come to Iraq, however. Saddam Hussein's army continued its brutal advance on the Kurdish north. After Saddam's forces rained artillery shells and aerial bombs on the region's cities, hundreds of thousands of panicked Kurds fled northward toward the mountainous areas along the border with Turkey and Iran before his ground troops swept through. Iraqi helicopter gunships pursued them mercilessly.

The rugged mountains afforded some protection from attacks by the Iraqi army. But in the makeshift encampments of displaced Kurds, the situation was dire. Food was scarce, water sources quickly became contaminated, and clothing and shelter were inadequate against the frigid temperatures. People began dying.

Containing Saddam

On April 16, in the face of a looming humanitarian catastrophe, President Bush announced the establishment of "safe havens" in northern Iraq where relief supplies for the displaced Kurds would be distributed. To clear the way for the humanitarian aid effort, and to protect the Kurds from further aggression by Saddam's regime, a "no-fly" zone was established in northern Iraq. U.S., British, and French fighter pilots would patrol the skies north of the 36th parallel of latitude, shooting down any Iraqi aircraft that ventured into this no-fly zone.

These measures helped convince Saddam to end his offensive against the Kurds. Over the next dozen years, under the protection afforded by the no-fly zone, the Kurds established an autonomous area where they were essentially free from Baghdad's control. Although another no-fly zone was established in Iraq south of the 32nd parallel in August 1992 (and was expanded to the 33rd parallel four years later), Saddam's repression of the Shia remained severe.

Although Saddam never mounted a serious military challenge to the no-fly zones, minor hostile incidents did occur with some frequency. Iraqi missile batteries often locked their radar onto U.S. or British planes, and Iraqi antiaircraft artillery was sometimes fired. In such cases pilots patrolling the no-fly zones typically fired back at the Iraqi installations on the ground.

For the United States and its allies, such incidents were an unwelcome reminder of Saddam's continued defiance, but of more concern was the status of Iraq's WMD programs. Saddam had agreed to give teams of United Nations weapons inspectors unimpeded access to military installations and research facilities throughout the country to verify Iraq's compliance with its disarmament obligations. Yet the UN inspectors continually found their work thwarted by the Iraqis, despite ongoing economic sanctions designed to elicit Iraq's full cooperation. As the years passed, the sanctions became increasingly controversial because of the harsh toll they took on the Iraqi people. The UN set up a program whereby Iraq was permitted to sell

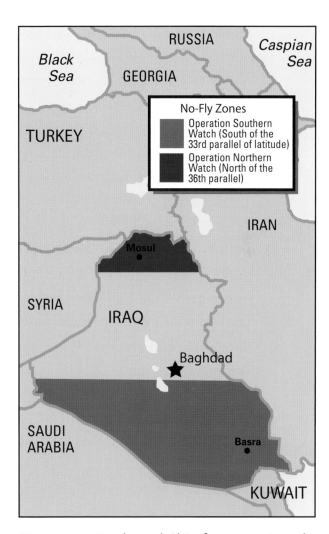

To protect Kurds and Shia from continued aggression at the hands of Saddam Hussein's regime, the United States and its allies established "no-fly" zones in northern and southern Iraq.

some of its oil for food and medicine, but Saddam managed to divert funds from the oil sales to support his regime.

In 1998 the UN weapons inspectors were pulled out of Iraq, and U.S. and British forces undertook a three-day bombing campaign to destroy suspected weapons research and production sites. Only after the 2003 U.S.-led invasion that toppled Saddam's regime would it become clear that Iraq's weapons of mass destruction had in fact already been eliminated.

Tensions Among the GCC States

Saddam's invasion of Kuwait had exposed the deep hostility of many Arabs toward the rich states of the Gulf Cooperation Council. Yet the Gulf War had seen the six GCC states join with Egypt and Syria in the anti-Iraq coalition, a development that seemed to portend greater cooperation between Arab rich and poor. After the war, however, the Arab alliance quickly faded. In part, this was because the GCC states were unwilling to entrust their security to other Arab countries that had opposed them in the past.

Despite the liberation of Kuwait and the decisive defeat of Iraq's armed forces, Saddam remained at least a potential threat to the GCC states. Similarly, while Iran had been seriously weakened by its long war with Iraq, the Sunni monarchies of the Gulf continued to be concerned by the intentions of the Islamic Republic's Shia mullahs.

Thus the Gulf countries remained dependent on Western power for their protection. The rulers and their families strengthened their alliances with the United States, which they permitted to store more equipment and operate military units in their countries. The U.S. Navy used Bahrain as the center of its operations in the Gulf. The American, British, and French aircraft that patrolled the southern no-fly zone in Iraq flew their missions from bases in Saudi Arabia. After the Gulf War, in fact, several thousand U.S. military personnel were stationed permanently in Saudi Arabia.

Although the people of the GCC states were generally friendly to the West, many were uncomfortable with the close security relationship their countries had with the United States. In their view, Gulf rulers often were coerced or enticed into doing Washington's bidding, without regard for the best interests of their own people. In addition, many Arabs in the Gulf countries deeply resented certain U.S. policies, particularly Washington's support for Israel in its conflict with the Palestinians. Many also came to oppose the continuing economic sanctions against Iraq, believing that the measures were causing unconscionable suffering for the Iraqi people. Some Gulf Arabs even considered the sanctions a deliberate effort by the United States and Europe to keep the Arab world weak by crippling Iraq.

Among Saudis, resentment of the United States—and of the Saudi monarchy—was especially significant. Between the mid-1980s and the mid-1990s, the average Saudi citizen saw his income decline by about three-fourths, in part because of flat oil revenues, in part because of a rapidly growing population, and in part because of the predatory ways of the corrupt royal family. Religious tensions also fractured the kingdom. Some Saudis believed that the Al Saud monarchy had betrayed Islam. Especially infuriating to Saudi Arabia's most conservative Muslims was the presence of "infidel" American soldiers in the land of the prophet Muhammad. That grievance would be cited as one of the justifications for the jihad against the

In the years after the Gulf War, Islamic fundamentalists chafed at the continued presence of American armed forces in Saudi Arabia. On June 25, 1996, terrorists detonated a massive truck bomb at the Khobar Towers residential complex in Dhahran. The blast destroyed the building in this photo, killing 19 American airmen and wounding more than 370 Americans and Saudis.

United States carried out by the Islamist terrorist organization al-Qaeda. Al-Qaeda would also call for the overthrow of the Saudi monarchy and would carry out attacks inside Saudi Arabia.

Developments in Iran

Throughout the post–Gulf War period, Iran remained a nemesis of the United States, which regarded the Islamic Republic as a potential threat to the safety of oil routes, to the security of its GCC allies, and to other U.S. interests in the region. After the death of Iran's Supreme Leader, Ayatollah Ruhollah Khomeini, on June 3, 1989, the Shia clerics' tight control over Iranian society was briefly loosened. But ultimately Khomeini's passing failed to dramatically alter Iran's conservative theocracy or its anti-Israel, anti-U.S. posture. Iran sponsored the Shia extremist groups Hamas and Hezbollah, which carried out a bombing campaign against Israeli targets in Israel, the Palestinian territories, and Lebanon. Iran was also suspected of involvement in several attacks on U.S. targets in the Middle East. Its alleged sponsorship of terrorism left Iran isolated diplomatically.

On the surface at least, the power of Iran's clerical leaders appeared firmly entrenched, and their goals as uncompromising as had been those of Ayatollah Khomeini. Yet Iran experts wondered whether the Islamic Revolution would endure in the face of various external and internal pressures. Although the Gulf War had dramatically reduced the threat from Iraq, and Iran had regained important rights in the Shatt al Arab waterway, Iran's economy remained hobbled by debt, damage to its industry and loss of workers sustained in the war with Iraq, and continuing U.S. restrictions on trade and investment. Equally important, popular dissatisfaction with the mullahs was apparently fairly widespread in Iran, especially among the country's growing ranks of young people.

In Iran, as in the rest of the Gulf, uncertainty followed the turbulent years between the Islamic Revolution and the Gulf War.

1918: Great Britain assumes control of the new state of Iraq under a League of Nations mandate.

1932: The Kingdom of Saudi Arabia is created.

1961: Britain deploys armed forces to Kuwait to prevent a possible Iraqi attack.

1971: Britain withdraws politically and militarily from its position in the Gulf; the smaller states of the Gulf receive their full independence.

1979: In January, in the midst of growing unrest, Shah Mohammad Reza Pahlavi leaves Iran. In February Ayatollah Ruhollah Khomeini returns to Iran after years in exile; he assumes the title of Supreme Leader of the Islamic Revolution. In April, with supporters of the shah defeated, Khomeini proclaims the creation of the Islamic Republic of Iran. In November militant Iranian students storm the American embassy in Tehran and take diplomats and staff hostage.

1980: In July the exiled shah dies. In September Iraqi forces invade neighboring Iran, triggering the Iran-Iraq War.

1981: In January Iran finally releases the American hostages in Tehran.

1987: After the Iran-Iraq War expands to shipping in the Gulf, 11 Kuwaiti oil tankers are "reflagged" as American vessels to deter Iranian attacks.

1988: Ayatollah Khomeini agrees to a cease-fire that brings the eight-year-long Iran-Iraq War to an end.

1990: Saddam Hussein, the Iraqi dictator, repeatedly complains about the Arab Gulf states' unwillingness to forgive Iraq's war debts and accuses Kuwait and the United Arab Emirates of carrying out "economic warfare" against his country by exceeding their petroleum production quotas. In July he charges that Kuwait has been stealing oil from the Iraqi side of the Rumaila oil field along the two countries' border. Egyptian and Saudi attempts to mediate the Iraq-Kuwait dispute fail, and on August 2 Iraq invades Kuwait. In a series of Security Council Resolutions, the United Nations condemns the invasion, imposes economic sanctions on Iraq, and demands the immediate and unconditional withdrawal of Iraqi forces from Kuwait. Concerned that Saddam might be planning an invasion of his country, King Fahd requests that a U.S. military force be deployed to protect Saudi Arabia. U.S. leaders build a large multinational coalition, including Arab states, to protect Saudi Arabia and ultimately to liberate Kuwait. In December the United Nations sets January 15 as the deadline for a full Iraqi withdrawal from Kuwait.

1991: The Gulf War begins on January 17 with aerial attacks on Iraq and on Iraqi positions in Kuwait; the air phase of Operation Desert Storm, the U.S.-led coalition's campaign to expel Iraq from Kuwait, lasts more than five weeks. Operation Desert Storm's ground war begins on February 24. Iraqi forces are quickly routed and Kuwait is liberated before U.S. president George H. W. Bush announces a cease-fire, which goes into effect on February 28. Encouraged by President Bush, Shia in southern Iraq and Kurds in the north rebel against Saddam's regime, but these uprisings are ruthlessly quelled. The United States, Great Britain, and France begin enforcing a no-fly zone in northern Iraq to protect Kurds from Saddam's forces (a similar no-fly zone is imposed the following year in southern Iraq to protect the Shia). A permanent Gulf War cease-fire goes into effect on April 11; among the terms Iraq accepts—but, according to critics, does not fulfill—is the destruction of its weapons of mass destruction (WMD) and the dismantling of its WMD programs.

Arab—a member of an Arabic-speaking, predominantly Muslim people originating in the Arabian Peninsula who today form the majority population in 21 countries of the Middle East, in addition to Palestine.

ayatollah—an important and revered religious leader among Shia Muslims.

emir—the title of the ruler in Kuwait, Qatar, and the United Arab Emirates, from an Arabic word meaning "prince."

faqih—the Supreme Leader of the Iranian Revolution.

Islam—a monotheistic religion that today claims more than a billion adherents worldwide and that originated on the Arabian Peninsula in the seventh century A.D. with the teachings of the prophet Muhammad.

Kurd—a member of a predominantly Sunni Muslim people who live in the mountainous area shared by Iraq, Iran, Turkey, and Syria and who speak a language similar to Persian.

mullah—a Muslim religious official or cleric, especially in Iran.

Muslim—a follower of Islam.

OPEC—the Organization of Petroleum Exporting Countries, a group of 11 countries from the developing world that export large amounts of oil and have agreed to coordinate their levels of production.

Ottoman—relating to a Turkish Islamic empire that controlled much of the Middle East from the 16th to the early 20th century.

Persian—relating to any of the various civilizations and empires that developed on the territory of modern-day Iran, which was referred to as Persia before the 20th century; the majority language in Iran (also known as Farsi).

shah—a ruler of Iran before the 1979 revolution, from the Persian word for "king."

Shatt al Arab—the waterway that is formed by the Tigris and Euphrates Rivers in Iraq and that flows into the Gulf.

Shia—the smaller of Islam's two major branches, whose rift with the larger Sunni branch originated in seventh-century disputes over who should succeed the prophet Muhammad as leader of the Muslim community.

Sunni—a Muslim who belongs to the largest branch of Islam.

Wahhabism—a highly conservative form of Sunni Islam practiced in Saudi Arabia.

Bill, James A. *The Eagle and the Lion: The Tragedy of American-Iranian Relations*. New Haven, Conn.: Yale University Press, 1988.

Chadwick, Frank, and Matt Caffrey. *Gulf War Fact Book*. Bloomington, Ill.: GDW, 1991.

Congressional Quarterly. *The Middle East*, 10th ed. Washington, D.C.: Congressional Quarterly, 2005.

Hiro, Dilip. *Desert Shield to Desert Storm: The Second Gulf War*. London: HarperCollins, 1992.

Keddie, Nikki R., with Yann Richard. *Roots of Revolution: An Interpretive History of Modern Iran*. New Haven, Conn.: Yale University Press, 1981.

Long, David E. *The Kingdom of Saudi Arabia*. Gainesville: University Press of Florida, 1997.

Marr, Phebe. *The Modern History of Iraq*, 2nd ed. Boulder, Colo.: Westview, 2004.

Metz, Helen Chapin, ed. *Persian Gulf States*. Washington, D.C.: Library of Congress, 1994.

———, ed. *Saudi Arabia: A Country Study*, 5th ed. Washington, D.C.: Library of Congress, 1993.

Summers, Harry G. *Persian Gulf War Almanac*. New York: Facts On File, 1995.

Tripp, Charles. *A History of Iraq*. Cambridge, UK: Cambridge University Press, 2000.

http://english.aljazeera.net/

The English website of Al Jazeera, the controversial television network based in Qatar.

https://www.cia.gov/cia/publications/factbook/index.html

The CIA World Factbook provides a wealth of background and statistical information on all the world's countries.

http://gulf2000.columbia.edu/

Created by the Gulf 2000 Project at Columbia University, this website provides basic information on all the Gulf states, as well as many links and bibliographies.

http://www.grc.ae/

The website of the Gulf Research Center, a private organization in Dubai (UAE) devoted to providing information on the Gulf.

http://www.middle-east-online.com/english/

Middle East Online, a website providing comprehensive and objective news reports on the region.

http://link.lanic.utexas.edu/menic/

The Middle East Network Information Center, from the University of Texas, provides information, links, and maps.

Numbers in **bold italic** refer to captions.

Contributors

Dr. J. E. Peterson has taught Middle East politics at several universities. He has been associated with a number of research institutes and has done extensive research and worked in the Gulf. He has published nearly a dozen books on the region and more than 40 scholarly articles.

Picture Credits